SINCE 2021

Toronto, Ontario, Canada

This Book Belongs To:

_____

_____

_____

Decaf

THE ULTIMATE

OXYMORON

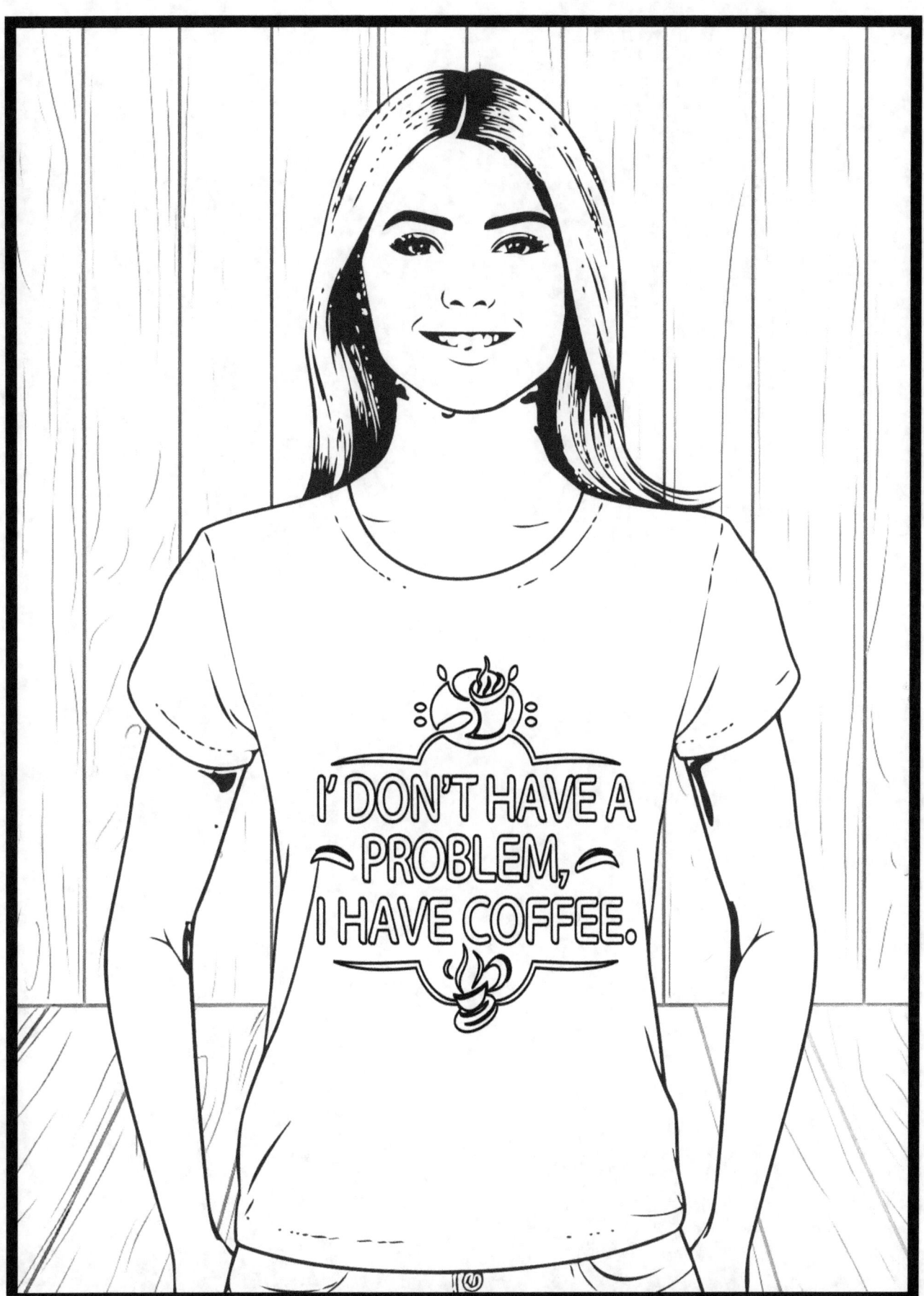

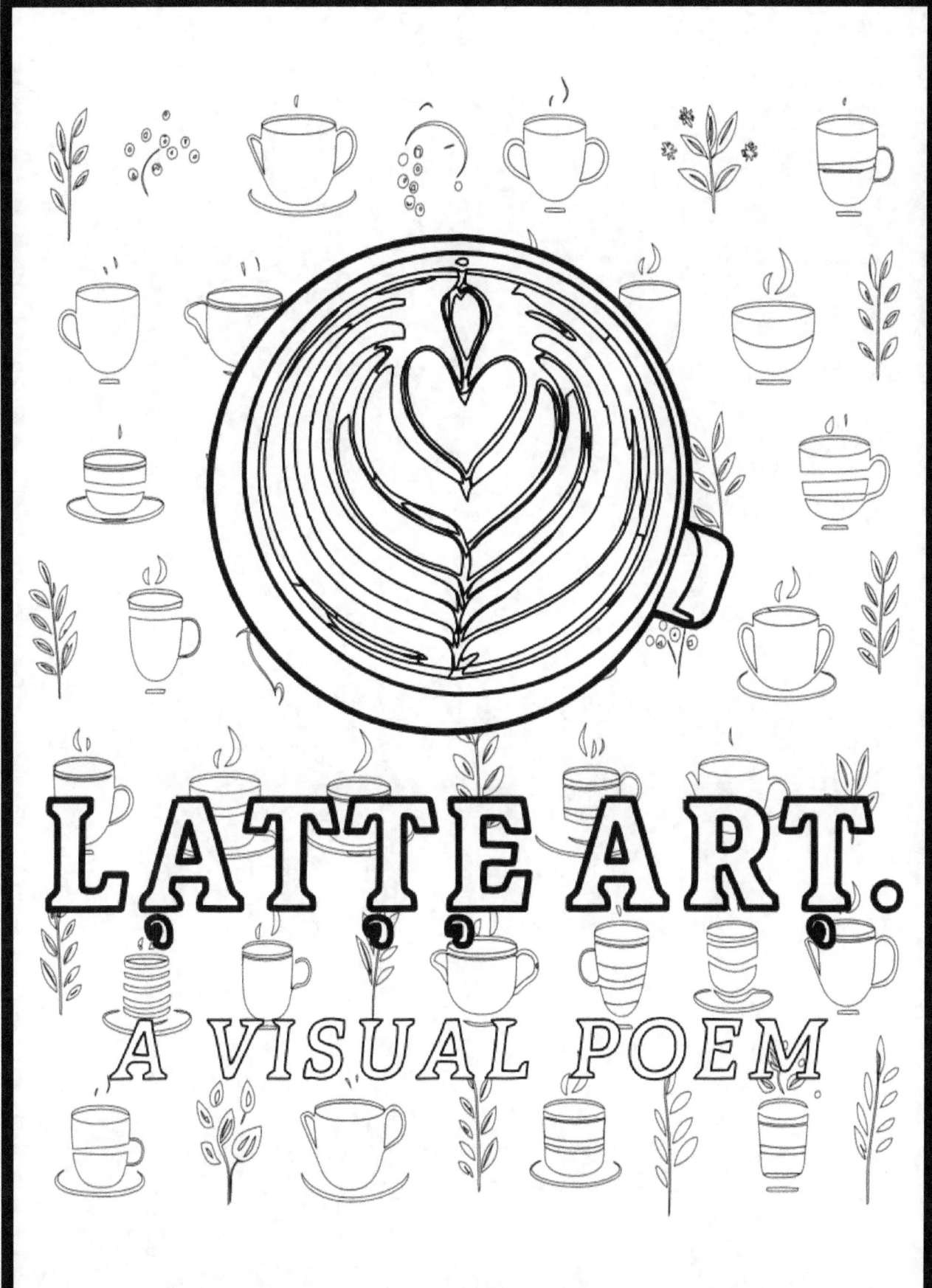

LATTE ART.

A VISUAL POEM

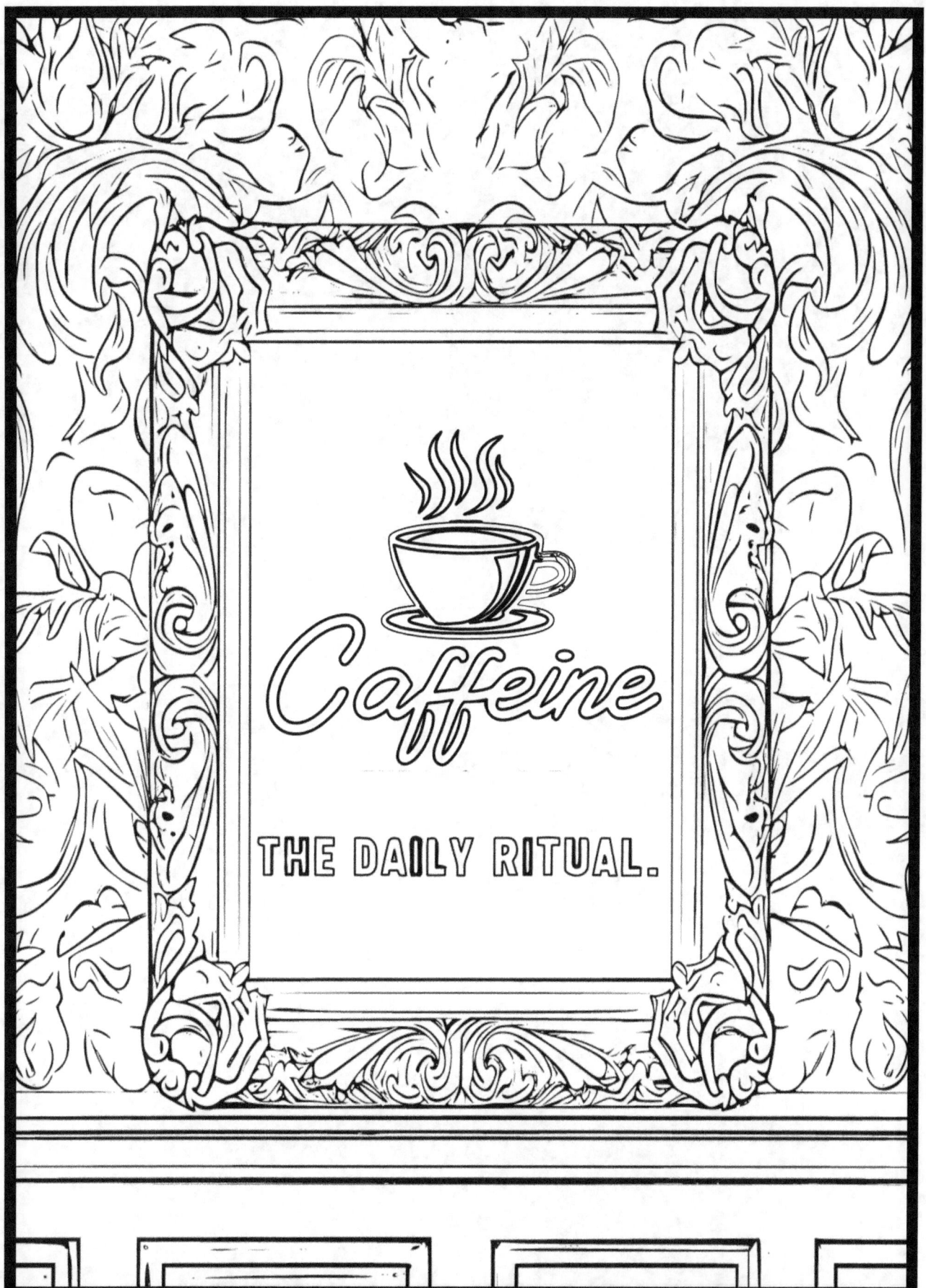

www.ingramcontent.com/pod-product-compliance
Lightning Source LLC
Chambersburg PA
CBHW081005120626
46546CB00010B/3021